BIRDHOUSE CC.....

Hume Cronyn

Keep writing and may I hear or See
you work at sometime
Love hume

SOWDANCY

Acknowledgements are due to the editors of the following magazines in which some of these poems first appeared: *Scratch*, *Slow Dancer*, *New Directions*, *The Echo Room*, *The Wide Skirt*, *Ambit*, and *Graffiti*; also to Mosaic Press for permission to publish four poems from **Bake My Brain**.

Published by **Slow Dancer Press**
58 Rutland Road, West Bridgford
Nottingham NG2 5DG

Slow Dancer is a member of the Association of Little Presses and gratefully receives financial support from East Midlands Arts.

ISBN 1 871033 225

CONTENTS

CHRISTMAS BLUES

When the snow lies in patches on my easy chair,
when my room grows stuffy like a herd of deer,
when Christmas hangs down my back like a wet tongue,
I flee from my room, I walk through parking lots,
inhale the sweet perfume of aluminium carbide,
trudge under bridges kicking at frozen puddles,
snap off the jovial moods growing from my shoulders,
scatter them like weeds,
I wail till the stray cats line up in procession behind me,
and when I come across Santa I beat him with a pack of chewing gum,
leave him an ironing board to dissect the dishonesty of his ways,
wrap him in nudity to protect him from the snakes,
warn him about the gold leaf that rots the tree,
refrigerate the sob that explodes from his hot burly body,
he understands like a splinter from a broken mirror,
thanks me for my birdhouse contributions,
while tears freeze on his cheeks like fences,
I call my cats, they come down from the birches,
with salty tongues, they lick the fences from his face,
I point out that the manger and the three wisemen have failed,
what comes down the chimney goes up in smoke,
sometimes white hair equals snow,
but I'll look for Christmas elsewhere.

ROLLED

If a man breaks you in two
and wants three pieces.

If a man pries open your throat
and pours down a crown of thorns.

If a man pulls the children from your eyes
and stuffs your sockets with a barren sky.

If a man drags a train through your belly
and talks about the redemption of walking.

If a man plants a bed of fatigue in your forehead
and salts the wind with one, and only one, truth.

If a man pulls a tree from your lungs
and crumples a few dead leaves in your pocket.

If a man wraps your love in a white-hot fist
and hocks it at the first pawnshop of the lamb.

If a man marches a procession of words over your tenderness
and proclaims that it is the army of healing.

If a man regales you with the laws of the holy city
and wrings the flowers like a dirty sponge.

If a man takes your sea and fills it with sand
and breaks the mast of your sailboat.

You know he's talking about God and eternal salvation,
the seven deadly sins and the testament of revenge.

You know he's talking about eternal forgiveness,
eternal damnation, the all-embracing love of God.

Omniscient! Omnipotent! Omnipresent! Beyond dispute!
Beyond comprehension! Beyond common sense! Beyond life!

You know that when you burst out screaming,
when you carry your head under your arm,

when you tear out your heart with nail clippers,
you know you've been rolled by one of God's messengers.

I PLAY AT HOUSE

My girlfriend is away,
I play at house.

The plates stack up in columns,
I hang feathers from the ceiling.

I water the flowers with milk,
Keep angelfish in the blender.

I float red balloons through the rooms,
Spin spider webs from balls of wool.

Carrots rot in the candlesticks,
Birds roost in the fridge.

I plant forget-me-nots in her shoes,
Cover the staircase with tin foil.

I toast marshmallows for breakfast,
Wash my clothes in her perfume.

I bury the alarm clock in pancake batter,
Grow dandelions in our bed.

I paint measles on the bathroom mirror,
Wrap my sandwiches in her stockings.

I paint the walls with her make-up,
Dress all the chairs in her blouses.

DEAR K

I sleep on your side of the bed
in your pink sweat shirt.
Your green sweater sleeps beneath my head.
Every night I take a jar of water to bed.
I have arranged your plants around the bed,
and when I can't sleep
I reach over and water them.
(You say we should starve each other,
sex has become too important.)
I see you in the clear curve of water.
I love the smell of damp earth.

Last night I dreamed of an old friend.
We talked about his older brother,
who died several years ago.
When I awoke,
I remembered his brother was alive:
it was he who was dead.

Today I got your postcard:
the 'Provosts Bell' of Trinity college.
The caption says it rings three times
when the Provost crosses the Front Square.
Three times is a famine!
When we're together,
I tremble with bells.
(Sometimes I think you do also.)
I've done nothing today:
I keep playing Dylan's 'Corrina, Corrina'
and stare at your card.
There's a word I can't make out
— the postmark has obscured it —
I tilt the card this way and that,
squint my eyes,
but I still can't read it.
(I think I've punctured my eardrum,
sometimes I lose my balance.)
If only you would whisper the word into my ear.

I'm always eating:
millet and green peppers,
peaches and bananas,
fig and orange cake,
and lots of coffee.
I'm starving.

8

I have no younger brother.
(He's dead because he was never born.)
Since I've met you,
he grows inside.
Soon he will be taller than me.
He needs the clear curve of your water.

I love the smell of you beside me.
When we do not starve each other,
a forest towers above us.

DOUG

He called the gutter
his private supermarket.

The objects that he found,
he called INTS

for interesting.

He had a special fascination
for screws.

He mounted them on cardboard
in columns

according to their personality:
the fat man,

the jolly,
the depressed,
the outrageous,
the flamboyant,

the pretty,
the quarrelsome, etc.

An old pen,
he would mount on a pile of books

and pretend
it was a spaceship

that after death
he would sail the galaxies in.

Bottletops,
creased by their opening,

he would hang them from strings —

prehistoric birds
that floated above his bed.

Matches,
he kept in a box,

firewood
for after the holocaust.

The pits of cherries
were planets

he carried around
in his pockets.

An inch-high plastic doll
with a sun bonnet that

dwarfs her

is his future wife
in heaven,

their many arguments
he has already dreamt.

A stone
that has the face of an Egyptian,

he places on

a passage in the bible
to guarantee
the survival of his supermarket.

COFFEE WITH DOUG

From the window of Finger's Donut Shop,

you and I look out. We sit
in plastic seats, drink cold coffee,
the occasional bite from a day-old donut.

Years ago you had burnt a third eye into your forehead
with a red-hot stone, thinking you were God.
In and out of hospitals, for years sleeping on the
glassed-in veranda of your boarding house —
friends would pray you'd make it through the winter nights.

You start the conversation, talk about the satellite dish across the street,
wonder about those who live below it, whether
they are receptive to the tremors it sends to their subconscious?

We throw pieces of donut to the pigeons in the doorway.
One is pure white. You talk about
childhood, nursing wounded pigeons in an attic room.
You tell me about tiplers and rollers and homing pigeons:
one flies in circles, one somersaults through the air, one carries
     messages.

I watch the wind through the trees.
In one, it seems to soothe;
in another, it is angry and ravaging.

You point out the maple tree at the corner,
how one day you were stunned to see its green leaves sprinkled with
     yellow;
it was early summer, and as you stood there,
a wind rifled through the tree, tore every
yellow leaf from its limbs.

We talk about the apartment building down the street
— built in the fifties, already dilapidated —
you point out how they are tarring the roof,
how the metal frame at the roof's edge
looks like a whaler's harpoon, how the orange wheelbarrow
that they are lowering from it, hundreds of feet,
contains the unhatched eggs of tonight's dreams.

Then you tell me how Steve has moved out from your boarding house
    to live with Sharon,
how they leave scraps of meat and bowls of milk in deserted garages,
how they walk on window ledges when they are drunk,
how Steve always carries in his shirt pocket a stone that looks like an
    ear.

You tell me about the front door that is never used at your place,
about the side door and the eavestrough that was repaired
— how things are looking up for you —
now when it's raining you can enter the side door
without a gush of water soaking you.

And then you mention lunch, you have to be home at noon.
And you return to your cupboard-size room and I, ablaze,
take a streetcar across the city, return to work.

STRANDED

Between the wall with leaves dropping like hearts and the desk that smells like a tired old root, I have followed the nightman. If it was not for his hats, worn out as the moon, and the leg that he left behind in the oozing mud — now hard as cement — I would have lost him years ago.

Not that you'd be proud of me. Most of the time I spend sitting in white chairs. Sometimes you'll find me hiding under them. I hate myself when I start eating the carpet.

My quest is for the floorboards. It's such a waste to ignore the wonderful gift of bare feet. We were born to have the rough taste of wood rub up against our toes. Of course I don't underestimate the chance of slivers.

And it doesn't help that my fingernails are pared so close to the quick.

If you were perceptive, and sometimes even I miss it when I look in the mirror, you'll see that I have a collection of small droplets beneath my eyes.

No matter how small you are, they are not deep enough to dive into.

So fuck you, nightman! I feel as if I'll always be stranded in this desert. So what if you've left me your leg, like a signpost in the dry and cracked mud.

What good is it? I need two legs to walk to the lake with mirror-like stones.

SHADOW MAN

In the evening when the grass lies down like a rotting pair of pyjamas

the man with the shaved head and the vagrant look arises from his bed with 2000 years of make-up and a crown with several names

he has bells on his shoes and a history of bad mistakes, and his pockets, which have no room for his hands, one of them bulges with a change purse full of bottle tops

he has no pretensions, he wanders midst the sirens and the skid row streetlife that never sleeps

he carries a garbage bag full of statues and hymn books, and cadges cigarettes as regular as a car pulls over to pick up a red skirt

cats play in his sleeve, sparrows nest in his matchbox, he lights his cigarette with a bee

he has become transcendent, transcendent as a whiff of smoke

and his hair eaten away by the streets, his teeth eaten like the windows of derelict buildings, his tongue a swollen carp, his eyes so many murdered tomorrows

he — I recognize him — he walks behind me

Get away! Get away!

IN MY HOUSE

I carry laughter in my back pocket.
I carry it from room to room because
there are no lightbulbs. At times,
laughter is better than electricity,

then it wilts like an old cherry,
and I'm left with a pit of darkness.
I crawl to the basement, try to find
my old pair of shoes. It's not easy.

Sometimes they are buried beneath the apples,
sometimes in the coal, once or twice
I've found them hanging from the water pipes.
Many times, they're impossible to find.

Still, I try to be patient,
because when I do find them,
I open up their tongues, slip them on
— their laces never the same colour twice —

then I don't need light, I don't need dark,
I can walk up the stairs of my house,
I just glide, and the stairs are transparent,
and the banisters are sunlight, and

the few times I have passed through the roof,
I have been the sky and light, and all
the misery and happiness that humans endure.
For a minute, I have felt totally alive.

PEARS

Please don't disturb!
A man in here
Is eating some lettuce
And a fruit
With the most delicate ears.

Pears
Hear everything that is said.
They must be eaten in silence.

With a knife
Cut stairs
That wind around the pear.
Walk up the stairs
With a candle:
The flicker of light
Is lost in the white pulp.
Nothing is seen.
Nothing is heard.
All is taste.

Taste
That sweeps through the body,
Grows larger than the body,
Encloses
The body in one large pear.

Shhh!
That man is a pear.
Few people know such a delight.

SUBURBAN PANIC

i'm in the backyard
i'm reading a book beneath the tree
a birdhouse is perched on a pole
a cat stalks through the grass
a bird screams so loud i want to run inside
from behind a lawn chair a silver balloon flies up like a boxing glove
water from the sprinkler is thrown into my face
someone crashes into their pool
the leaves of the maple tree rustle with a tinny sound
the grass is sharp on my bare feet
roller skates sit on the patio table   swamped
by the shade of the mushroom-coloured umbrella
rust grows on the teeter totter
a tremendous bruising sound
a family of sparrows fly into the air
i trip over a tricycle
scratch myself
i'm on my hands and knees   feeling
the stubs of a hacked-down bush
the leaves are perforated
the water from the sprinkler dies
the bird screams
i can't get inside   the walls are transparent
i know there's a door
my fingernails break on glass
i knock into a watering can
i can't find the door
the birdhouse blows over
something hits my back
i'm

AROUND THE POOL

Airplanes fly back and forth tugging a string of letters with
　　　advertisements such as CONFETTI RED HOT REGGAE PARTY
　　　TONITE. LADIES DRINKS FREE. You can only read the letters
　　　in one direction.
A man gets out of the pool in a bathing suit that looks like a lime-green
　　　diaper, goes over to his girlfriend, shakes his wet hair all over
　　　her, she goes inside and gets his lime-green sunglasses.
A little girl in the pool holds up a sailboat with red sails, 'Mummy, can
　　　I get out?' Mummy, sprawled on a deck chair, the *Miami Herald*
　　　covering her like a beach towel, is sound asleep.
I'm sitting on the patio of our hotel room, a low hedge separates me
　　　from the bathers around the pool, the waves of the ocean are
　　　drowned out by the rinse cycle of the dishwasher, my
　　　mother-in-law is talking to a lizard.
The wind tears at the flags of five countries, but the tops of the royal
　　　palms are barely moving.
Every few minutes a bather sits up and vigorously slathers on more sun
　　　tan lotion.
Some very fat bodies have stepped into bikinis and are wisely lying
　　　down.
Even men in their twenties have paunches.
The ceaseless drone of airplanes.
A sand crab scoots under my chair heading for the open door, but
　　　when he takes his first step onto the carpet, my mother-in-law
　　　whacks him with a newspaper.
The pregnant woman appears earlier than usual, I have never seen a
　　　woman look so sad in pregnancy, but today she takes off her
　　　sand-coloured pullover, revealing a bathing suit of the subtlest
　　　marine-blue with a flamboyant red bow.
A helicopter flies overhead, two children run as if they were going to
　　　hit the deck, a little boy drops his pail.
My wife and daughter stand at the gate, they have returned from the
　　　beach, they dip rags in turpentine and scrub off oil that wodges
　　　up between toes, cakes heels, streaks legs, spots hands.
The sand crab has moved next door, a little girl pokes it with a stick,
　　　her mother says, 'Don't, you must be kind to the fish and
　　　crustaceans. They were here before we were.'
A lizard darts under the hedge, plates clatter as my mother-in-law starts
　　　to unload the dishwasher, I bury my head in a biography of a
　　　Russian poet.

GIDDY-UP

Grandma sits in her easy chair.
In a blue chiffon dress,
immaculately lipsticked,
she reads her romance.

Her two grandsons ride
the back of her couch.
'Giddy-up,' they shout, 'GIDDY-UP.'

Grandma reads her romance.
She is waiting for her dead husband's
brother to pick her up for dinner.

Her granddaughter, on the other side of the room,
has pulled on her ice skates, is tying up
the laces.

Grandma reads her romance.

Her daughter kneels in front of the fireplace,
hypnotically watches the kindling burst into flames.
She has just had an argument with her husband.

Grandma sips from her tea,
then sinks back into her romance.

One of her grandsons is about to fall off the couch,
her granddaughter to stand up and walk across the rug in her skates,
her daughter to plunge her hand into the fire.

Grandma, three pages from the end of her romance.

The boy falls off the couch,
smashes his head against the window.
The little girl skates across the rug.
The woman moves closer to the fire.

Grandma puts down her romance,
'In Patagonia they found true love.
They eloped, riding horses across the pampas.'

Her daughter stuffs a newspaper into the fire.
Tomorrow they'll take the kids to the zoo.

RED AND GREEN

The dishes are piled.
The children are in the living room.
We talk in the falling light.

Talk about.

Chloe and her first week of school.
How tired we are. The cost of a monthly pass.
Who's going to phone the repairman?
What are we going to do for Phil's fortieth?

The screech of trains fills the room.
A lightbulb shines brightly, then goes out.
The tap is dripping. The picture on the wall
is losing its detail in the growing dark.

With nothing on but a diaper,
Blake appears at the end of the hall,
runs towards us,
whooping with delight,
ee-ai ee-ai ee-ai

when he reaches the kitchen,
he turns, runs back down the hall,
two pairs of mittens are
caught around his foot
— mittens on strings —

they bounce up and down
red and green
bounce up and down
ee-ai ee-ai ee-ai

red and green

green and red

commas to an ongoing sentence,
while you and I, slumped in chairs,
are caught in full stops.

LOVE POEM

The Nick Cave look-alike with hair black as gloss paint sitting beside the girl with the studded dog collar around her neck, the young woman in the flower-print dress with three gladiolas lying on her lap, the woman reading a Harlequin romance while her other hand steadies a gold-framed picture of a pit bull wearing a cowboy hat.

It's late at night, we are sitting on a bus, so many single people — only one couple — we are all delirious with the thought of going home alone, the air crackles, we are wrapped in sweat, there's the squeak-squeak of chewing gum, how many times we steal a glance.

And the bus waits in its bay, it waits, its sides are rattling, the smell of worn tires creeps in through the windows, and we wait while the bus driver is down in the subway station licking his fingers dripping from the oozing cinnamon roll that he has just bought.

We sit, the first wave of passengers to board the bus, we sit and watch as the second wave searches for their seats — the man whose tattooed hand grips a Dominion bag stuffed with celery and the cloudy smelling of cheese, the blonde with bare, pearl-white shoulders crossed by satiny black bra straps, the woman in her leopard-skin mini-skirt and velvet cowboy boots, although it's ninety outside,

and the man sitting across from me, with spit-shone penny loafers and a row of pens stuck in the pocket of his Brooks Brothers shirt, according to their height, who sits with all the self-importance of a Bay Street executive,

even he looks at her,

and the bus driver returns with the remainder of his cinnamon roll in a grease-stained paper bag, and the jaggery smell of cinnamon swirls down the aisle of the bus, and it hovers and nudges till our nostrils flare and our skins break out in goose bumps,

and the Caribbean woman who sits iconic with the silver hoops of her earrings shimmering, and the Portuguese woman who wears her gold earrings like treble clefs, and I who can't read a word of my book, *The Dynamics of Creation*,

we swirl in a sea of sexual currents,

and the seats of the bus, fiberglass and painted with brown squares to resemble cushions, even they, with all the suggestiveness of dirty dish water, are transformed — the tawny brown of lions, one hair of a camel, the pouch of a kangaroo — and on the seat next to me, two pennies sit side by side, and I cannot reach over and pick them up.

The bus drives, it drives through the night, past the neo-deco restaurants whose busboys are dragging out bags of garbage, past the 24-hour grocery stores, past the apartment blocks whose closet-size balconies advertise loneliness, into the heart of Lawrence Park,

the bus drives, and we are drawn: the punk girl with her head shaven except for a purple shank of hair that falls across her eyes, the woman in powder-blue socks and Donald Duck sweat-shirt, the man in Jesus sandals and faded T-shirt with dancing figures on it,

we are drawn into the same current, and as each one of us disembarks from the bus, all of us singly, except the punk couple, bare-armed and locking hands, chatting about coming down from an acid trip in the alleyway behind the organic butcher's,

each one of us watches with longing as the bus door clatters open, if only we had the nerve? the courage? the desperation? to ask if the departing person wanted company —

we imagine the walk home/the shy talk/the flick of a match to light a cigarette/the extraordinary expectation as keys are pulled from purse or pocket —

the bus door closes with a bang, one less person, and another, and another, till the sexual energy turns to emptiness, exhaustion grows,

and at the first stop after the bridge, the punk couple gets off, and I get off, I speed up and cross the road diagonally so that I don't get stuck behind them on the walk up the hill, I pass the house with the stately blue spruces, pass the house with the driveway of bricks, the house with two ponds,

and as I cross our lawn I notice that the garage door is slightly ajar, there's a sliver of light, it's one of those electric doors, I go to push the button but don't because the clattering of the mechanism might wake everyone in the house.

I pull out my keys, see that you've left the front door open, you pick your sleepy self up from the armchair in the living room, say that you've waited up for me, you thought I said I would phone from the subway station and that you'd have gladly picked me up. I said that I hadn't wanted you to wait up for me, I knew you were tired, I'm sorry we got our signals crossed, and anyways, I love the walk in, the houses along Glengowan,

and we sit on the floor of the bedroom, I vacantly stare at the dress you are wearing, it takes me a moment to recognize it, I haven't seen it for years, it's the dress which you wore when I first met you twenty years ago,

blue and cotton and pin-striped and simple with two pockets for your hands and the skewed collar which shows the fragile tent of your collarbone, so delicate your skin, almost transparent, the structure of those bones that will always take me further than any cathedral will,

and I remember our early years of necking in the back seats of cars, the time an old man jumped out from the bushes, the time two cops on horses knocked on our steamed-up windows at four in the morning, the first time I saw your breasts, the confusion that came over me when I saw three hairs sprouting from one of them,

and we talk about the children asleep in the bedroom, how Blake fell asleep on the living room floor at eight-thirty, how Koy counted up to twenty, about the growing attachment of Chloe and Grandma Teddy to the budgie found on the front lawn the other day, how rare it is that the children fall asleep before we do,

and your legs are drawn up yoga style, your legs are bare, the pink of your underwear shows, your fingers comb through your hair, pushing it off your forehead, then drop to take hold of the hem of your dress — stretched tautly between your knees like an open mouth — pinching it together so that your dress covers your underwear,

then you let go of the hem, mouth opens

I want you so much, twenty years, and I still want you, bursting through my clothes

through our skins.

24

MY BOOKCASE IS A BABY WHALE WITH 3000 TIGERS

For sixteen years I had my own room, a half-room, wide as I am tall, and maybe twice that length.
It was filled with books and records, two desks, a slew of art posters, and an old IBM typewriter.

A month ago I gave up my room to share with my four-year-old daughter, Chloe.
I still have a desk in the corner, and, along one of the walls, from one end to the other, stacked to the ceiling, orange crates filled with books.
Along the other wall, her bunk bed.

Chloe and I are sitting on the top bunk. We are reading Kenneth Lilly's ANIMALS.
We read that there are less than 3000 tigers left in the world.
I try to explain how few tigers that is; there's that many people living within a few blocks of us. And there's only that many tigers in the whole world!
She says, as many tigers as your books?
Yes, I laugh, each book is a tiger.

Then we read about the sperm whale; how the new-born are one of the world's largest babies, four metres long.
I tell Chloe that's about the length of my bookcase.
She says, your bookcase is a baby whale with 3000 tigers in its stomach.

Why didn't I give up my room earlier?

Hume Cronyn trained for business, taught Greek Mythology and Romantic Poetry at the City Lit (London), worked at a drop-in centre in the psychiatric ghetto of Parkdale, Toronto, now lives in London with his wife and three children. First full-length collection, **Bake My Brain** (Mosaic Press, Canada) is to appear in the spring of 1993.